Pebble in the Pond

Terry Dobson

Copyright © 2012 Terry Dobson

All rights reserved.

ISBN: 1477582894
ISBN-13: 978-1477582893

Dedication

To my Goddess and Muse who has gifted me with inspiration in my writing and my life. She makes my soul sing and I am ever loving and thankful.

Contents

Acknowledgements	i
New possibilities	1
Broken	2
Disaster	3
Chasing sheep	5
We're not dead yet	6
Darkest before dawn	7
Cries of the sea	8
My pagan rose	9
First date	10
Holistic Island	11
Pain	12
Ecstasy	13
Our tomorrow	14
Follow your path	15
Does it breathe?	16
Bring out your dead	17
Our journey	19
Whispers on the wind	22
Sands of time	23
Do not fear the dark	25
Lindisfarne	26
Perfect moment	27
What do you see?	28
Haunted	30
Silent screams	31
Our love	34
The hunt	35
There were always times	36
With open hearts	38
Sacrifice	39
Look at him now	40
Waking thoughts	41
Thoughts of the sea	42
Full moon rising	43
To love and light	44
Happy Valentine's Day	45

I offer myself	46
Blessed day	47
Was your love ever real	48
Love's light	50
The circle	51
Something beautiful	52
Didgeridoo	53
Rainbow of my heart	54
Heart laid bare	55
The way I feel	56
Footprints	57
Beach banks	58
Something happened to me	59
More than love	60
Rhythm of love	62
The face	63
The moon and you	64
The crystal	65
Prayer to you	66
A year of loving you	67
We and the moon	68
Spring in your eyes	69
Shadow and light	70
You are my Goddess	71

Acknowledgements

I would like to thank Mary Bell, Chris Robinson, Mavis Farrell, Agnes Frain, Rachael H. Dixon, Irene Styles and Brenda Graham, for their support over the years I have been a member of Easington Writers. I would also like to thank my aunt, Anne Dobson, for her encouragement, love and support throughout my life from the day I was born, and my sisters Vicki Kyle and Maria Cave. I must also mention my Reiki Master and mentor George Hollis who has been a blessing from the day I met him, and Carole Hollis, may she be blessed on the new stage in her life that she is embarking upon. I would like to thank my friends, including Michelle and Clair, the members of the Lindisfarne Retreat circle, and especially to Carole Briggs, who has given me much more than I could ever thank her for.

New possibilities

Trepidation stalks through my confused mind
Wary and watchful
An eye on my thoughts
New possibilities open in futures unexpected
Feelings long caged stretch their aching limbs
As they step slowly to freedom
Uncertain and cautious
They blink in the light
So many paths before them
They struggle to choose
With destiny unknown
She comes then
A catalyst for change
A pebble in the pond of my life
Ripples across the surface show the turmoil
That lies deeper
Reshapes and renews
And like those long-forgotten feelings
I stretch my aching limbs
Blink in the light
As I step from the darkness in which I've lived
Into a new dawn of hope

Terry Dobson

Broken

Shattered shards of sharp shiny daggers
Splintered on the floor
Lie in wait for unsuspecting feet
To walk through the kitchen door

Dawn breaks, birds welcome the day
Sudden high-pitched screams
As half-asleep feet descend
Waking in blood from shattered dreams

"That bloody cat!" the piercing words
Broken vase now tipped with red
A streak of black runs up the stairs
And vanishes beneath the still-warm bed

Disaster

It was just before dawn
That 29th of May
But no sirens shrieked
To give warning
Just cruel silence
That crept through empty streets
And peered in at unsuspecting windows
For one brief moment
Time stood still
Then a lorry sped by
Full of brave men
On their way
To where hell lay
In darkness
Buried within the coal
As minutes passed
Then hours
Word of mouth
Spread the news
An explosion underground
Crowds gathered
At Colliery gates
United in shock,
Horror, foreboding
81 men lost
The search goes on
Rescue work
Around the clock
Hundreds hold vigil
Into the third day
With hope fading fast
Tears and grief
Clutch at broken hearts
The mourning begins
A mass of sorrow
The death toll rises

Terry Dobson

Two rescuers join the 81
Here we are sixty years on
Each man still remembered
Their names inscribed
Carved in stone
Their trees stand tall
Rooted deep
Like those lost souls
They represent

Written to commemorate the sixtieth anniversary of the 1951
Easington Colliery Mining Disaster

Chasing sleep

Sleep evades me
It skips and giggles
Evading my grasp
Thoughts run through my mind
Clad in combat boots
Heavy and loud
Scream for attention
Demand to be heard
Even though I do not want to hear
All I want is to close my eyes
And wait for silence to fall
To succumb to unconsciousness
To forget for a while
The world and its woes
I want to slide into silent darkness
With no sight nor sound
Just perfect peace
In body and mind

Terry Dobson

We're not dead yet!

Empty houses, boarded windows
Sightless, lifeless piles of brick
No whistling, chattering, booted feet
Of men heading for their shift

Community spirit battered, shattered,
Shops closed, shutters down
Standing vacant, still and hoping
For better times to fill their shelves

Shrugging off the North Sea winds
We're made strong, hewn from the rock
Like the shafts sunk down below,
Proud that we're from mining stock

Children running, laughing, playing
Balls bouncing, people walking dogs
Marching onward to the future
Heads held high, no lowered eyes

So listen up, don't put us down
Don't count us out, we're on our feet,
We keep on moving, looking forward
To the future, we're not dead yet

First Published in *Shrugging Off the Wind: Tall Tales from Easington Writers*, edited by Wendy Robertson and Avril Joy, 2010

Darkest before dawn

Dark skies roil, black seas boil
Lighthouse broken, no safe harbour
Boat torn apart on storm washed rocks
Cling to wreck, hang on to life
Icy cold, shivers, taste of fear
Scared of being alone, left to die
In pain, with aching heart
Unloved and unwanted
But still hang on, a tiny spark of life
Body wracked, so tired and stressed
The screaming endless loneliness
Wait and hope the storm will pass
That night will fade, and sun will rise
That love will come, to hold, to heal
With warmth and comfort, to make life real
But how much longer can these empty arms
Keep holding tight to this wreck of life
That seems locked into this eternal storm
Before they let go and surrender all
And never see the longed for dawn

First Published in *Footprints at the Water's Edge: More Tales from Easington Writers*, edited by Terry Dobson, 2011

Terry Dobson

Cries of the sea

The sea, she whispers to me,
Her waves the breath of Mother Earth
From her depths she gave birth
To all of life
Now she's crying in pain
From the depredations of her children
The pollution that we've caused
Spread like a plague
Killing our Mother
We need to start now
To cleanse and to heal
To ease her pain
And hence our own
To learn to respect
And how we connect
To her, to each other
To one and to all

My pagan rose

I have been lost and wandering in the wilderness
Seeking but never finding
Thirsting but never drinking my fill
My pagan heart empty, aching, alone
Then I see my pagan rose blooming just out of reach
Calling out to me a siren song
My own heart betrays me, caught in a spell of my own making
I feel it fill once more, with emotions I am unready for
Like the moon pulling at the tides, I find myself drawn
My eyes damp as I reach out
And feel the thorns of my pagan rose pierce my heart
But the beauty of the flower is just beyond me
High upon its crown of thorns, tantalising
Its heady scent overpowering my senses
Sending me reeling to my knees
My soul burns and yearns
I weep with frustration, unknowing
As I search for the words, the key
And so I sit, waiting, hoping
For my pagan rose to come down to me
And yet not hoping at all, but so afraid
Of what I feel, could feel, alive once more
After all this time wandering, soulless, lost and empty
Should I brave those thorns once more
Ignore the pain, the aching
Or just sit and admire from afar
No great distance, but beyond the circle
Outside of the thorns
But within plain view, in time of her need
Or should I journey on through the wilderness
Seeking but never finding
Thirsting but never drinking my fill
My pagan heart empty, aching, alone

Terry Dobson

First date

First date
River bank
Slowly walk
Your hand in mine
Soft words
Gentle smiles
Shimmer of laughter
Bottle of wine
Ancient walls
Dark and grey
Like the sky
Tower high
Heart warm
Tender touch
Sunday joy
You and I

Holistic Island

Molten silver, cold and gleaming
Oozes over the tarmac
No stopping its relentless advance
And yet no feeling of being trapped
As I am enfolded in the tidal embrace
Surrounded not only by the cold North Sea
But by the warmth and love of friends
The presence of my Goddess and Muse
On this ancient island where we stand
Brings hope and light to my heart
And a smile to my face
Ten soul friends in a circle gather
Let go upon St. Cuthbert's Isle
Shed ourselves of unneeded burdens
Like cast off skin
No longer part of us
Just dead weight
Walk the path of the labyrinth
A symbol in the sand
Represents the twists and turns
That has brought us to our present
Each outstretched hand
Is taken up by another
No separation
Each part of the whole
A circle, living, loving
Cast in flesh and soul
With every strength and weakness
Balanced, supported, accepted
A holistic group of healers
Surrounded by love
And the cold North Sea

Terry Dobson

Pain

I tremble
The fear in my throat
Strangles me
Cuts off the air
I hear the music and laughter
On the other side of the wall
But I can't join in
Trapped in this darkness
The walls of my own creation
Keep everyone out
I retreat within my shell
The pain too intense
Cut off from everything
But the darkness in my soul
Hope ripped from me
Left bleeding in my nightmares
In some forgotten corner
Like an autumn leaf
Dried up and falling through the air
Discarded once again
Unwanted, unloved
To wither and rot away
Into nothingness

Ecstasy

Darkness, deep and soft
Silky black embrace
Caressing whisper
Warmth and strength
Tender in the night
Loving hearts
Invisible smiles
Fingertips sense
Unseen curve
Sharp inhale
Passion burns
Shaking touch
Skin on fire
Bodies ache
Gasping breath
Needs fulfilled
Souls entwined

Terry Dobson

Our tomorrow

A bitter sweet melancholy fills my heart
As music from my past haunts me
And echoes of my youth linger
Lost paths, lost loves, I bid them adieu
A weeping guitar brings a tear
That rolls slowly down my cheek
Then a gentle smile plays on my lips
As I recall a recent kiss
And I look to tomorrow with anticipation
My heart open and ready with hope
My hand outstretched to take yours
To look the future in the eye, together

Follow your path

Alone in the night, crying out loud in some nightmare.
Lost in the mist, knowing that there's something out there.
Haunted by fears and torments, what is the answer?
You believe that you know where to look, but you're running scared.

The stench of decaying civilisation surrounds you,
The rubble and chaos of life stands in your way,
Obstacles blocking your path, not to be shifted.
The Zombies are building their walls to persuade you to stay.

But if your thoughts are pure, and your conscience is clear,
Then you will find that there's nothing to fear.
Your instincts will find you the path you must tread
And then you can seek out the light up ahead.

Just follow your path, follow your soul,
Look into your heart to find your goal.
Open your mind to what your heart might teach
Then you will find the answer within your reach

Terry Dobson

Does it breathe?

Does a stone breathe?
We live on a rock
That needs air
To maintain life
The waves on the rocky shore
The breath of Mother Earth

Does a fire breathe?
It needs air
To feed it, fan it
Help it grow
To give it heat
To give it life

Does glass breathe?
It needs breath
To give it shape
To expand it
To give each piece beauty
To sparkle in the light

Does metal breathe?
Breath through a metal tube
Brings music
Creates a sonorous tone
That resonates in each ear
That listens

Bring out your dead

See her circle overhead
Her wings in glossy shades of night
Casting shadows across the battlefield
Ancient goddess of war and death
She becomes the wisdom of the crow
When you hear her call your fate is sealed

When your time comes she will appear
A feathered reaper of the dead
She'll ferry you to the Otherlands
Listen and you will hear her call
Whether you go peacefully in your own bed
Or in a pool of blood by another's hand

    Bring out your dead
    Bring out your dead
    The Morrigan is here
    Bring out your dead

    Bring out your dead
    Bring out your dead
    The Morrigan is here
    Bring out your dead

Her dark shape flies across the sky
A silhouette drawing ever near
A fate from which you can never run
She is neither evil nor unfeeling
She would not take your life
But one day she comes for everyone

As your soul slips from your flesh
She will gather you to her breast
And take you safely to the other side
She dwells within that sacred space
Between the spirit and the flesh
Gathering the souls of those who've died

Terry Dobson

> Bring out your dead
> Bring out your dead
> The Morrigan is here
> Bring out your dead
>
> Bring out your dead
> Bring out your dead
> The Morrigan is here
> Bring out your dead

Embrace her healing touch
Throw down your crutch
She will never hurt you
Nor will she desert you

Do not fear death
It is only loss of breath
An end to your pain
You will be born again

> Bring out your dead
> Bring out your dead
> The Morrigan is here
> Bring out your dead
>
> Bring out your dead
> Bring out your dead
> The Morrigan is here
> Bring out your dead
>
> Bring out your dead
> Bring out your dead
> The Morrigan is here
> Bring out your dead

Our journey

The bells rang out from the Cathedral
As we walked through the city
It was cold, but my hands were warm
That day in Durham
We sipped wine and nibbled cheese
As we sat by the river
Amused by the students rowing
Again and again into the bank
We sat on a comfy sofa
In the Oxfam bookshop
Where we admired the carved bookcase
So dark, so tactile and old
Tea with lemon in Vennel's
Then hunting for vintage treasures
A day spent walking, talking
Never lost for words
We arrived in York on crowded train
For the Viking Festival
We strolled through the railway museum
Hand in hand, lost in each other
Oblivious to crowds
Or the Hogwarts Express
And the children gathered there
To glimpse Dumbledore and Harry
And once again we could hear bells
Deep and mellow from the Minster
As we walked slowly through the Shambles
Laughing, chatting, smiling, happy
Seeking treasures in old shops
And then into a Festival tent
Filled with furs, so thick and soft
And jewellery, weapons, shields
And those pointed hats
For lunch we searched
For the pub with the pies!
But settled for a different place
We sampled Yorkshire Merlot
And vowed never again!

Terry Dobson

And then we saw the Deviant Moon
In the shop with a stock of Tarot cards
An old fashioned tea shop
It suited us well
Tea for two, with scone and jam
No phones allowed
Then Whitby, that day by the sea
Along the sandy beach
Where we saw the donkey rides
And strolled along the pier
We stood at the harbour entrance
And gazed upon the waves
Feeling the power and energy
Of the unremitting sea
And once again the bells were ringing
Echoing across from the opposite hill
Were we being stalked by bell ringers?
Three days, three dates, three places
A table top sale, we wandered in
Excited by the prospect of unknown treasures
A silver Goddess and a Viking-style pendant
Good finds, good buys, good eye
Walking up hills, meandering through shops
Looking for just the right ones
A little bit quirky, or vintage, or both
Plenty of those we found
Fish and chips, of course, for lunch
What else from such a seaside town
The time passing so quickly
Too quickly it seemed
More exploring, then another find
And another tea shop, so civilised
We sipped and talked some more
The last customers of the day
We return to the beach
Looking for stones
Then a steep climb to the top
Back to the car

Seaton Carew, as the full moon rose
With blankets and stove
And water for tea
We basked in the moonlight
We talked and we kissed
A magical night
Alone on the sand
Hand in hand
Each time so special
Each etched in my heart
May each time from now on
Be as magical
My beautiful muse
My Goddess, my lady
Each hour with you
Is treasure worth hoarding

Terry Dobson

Whispers on the wind

Voices
On the edge of hearing
You can't grasp their meaning
Like whispers on the wind

Stories
Hidden from your sight
Somewhere in the night
They're written on the wind

Rumours
Talk of some disgrace
They lie right to your face
They're running on the wind

Echoes
Bounce around the street
Then fading on repeat
Like whispers on the wind

Can you hear those whispers on the wind
Don't you listen to the whispers on the wind
They'll only lie to you
That's what they do

First Published in *Footprints at the Water's Edge: More Tales from Easington Writers*, edited by Terry Dobson, 2011

Sands of time

Maybe you remember when you said you loved me so
Maybe you remember it was not that long ago
But now your heart fills with shame
When you hear me call your name

Maybe you remember when we first made love
Maybe you remember when things were so good
But as our love grew older
You grew slowly colder
Then you went for blood

Now I'm drowning in a sea of sorrow
Will I live to see tomorrow
Will I ever live to love again
Sands of time keep on flowing
Winds of change keep on blowing
Help me to escape from all this pain

Sands of time, no friend of mine
Alone here with the beer and wine
Trying to forget the love I knew
Now you're gone I can't face it
Trying hard to replace it
But there'll never be another you

Maybe you remember walking hand in hand
Maybe you remember playing in the sand
But now it's just a memory
Now you are so far from me

Maybe you remember when you had to go
Maybe you remember when you hurt me so
You left me for another man
You left me to be damned
Why I just don't know

Terry Dobson

Why did you say goodbye?
Why did you make me cry?
Why did you break my heart in two?
Why did you have to leave?
Why did you have to deceive?
When you knew I loved you

Why did you have to lie?
Why did our love die?
Why did you run on out on me?
Sands of time please help me now
I can't escape I don't know how
I'm chained by my own misery

Sands of time be a friend to me
Sands of time set me free
Sands of time let me live again
Sands of time keep on flowing
Winds of change keep on blowing
Help me to escape from all this pain

Do not fear the dark

Curled in the darkness
Warm and safe
The darkness is not to be feared
For are we not born from darkness
No light shines in the womb
The moon in the night sky
Shining bright with the light of the reflected sun
And the darker the night
The brighter the stars
There is a balance
Shadow and light
Yin and Yang
Black and white
Do not fear the dark
Nor deny its presence
For without it how would we know
What the light means

Lindisfarne

I listen to the waves as they whisper to the sand
Tales of horror, of mystery, of the history of this land
Of stone age man who learnt to fish
And left behind unwanted rubbish
Of Aidan who from Iona came
And the Anglo Saxons he did tame
Of Cuthbert the healer who longed for peace
But people sought him without cease
Of the monks who lived and worked and prayed
Of the dragon ships that came to raid
Of the blood and death and frenzied theft
That left the island so bereft
And though Cuthbert had long been dead
With his body the people fled
Until the Vikings were no more
And the Normans came to this shore
The monastery was rebuilt
And the past buried in the silt
Until King Henry's Reformation
That almost tore apart the nation
I stand here gazing out to sea
This place now a part of me
Blessed and healed in the calm
Of the Holy Island of Lindisfarne

Perfect moment

I gaze into the night sky
A star catches my eye
And I realise that it's light
Has travelled many lifetimes
Just to be there in that perfect moment
For me to admire
And appreciate
You are the sun that lights my world
The moon that pulls at me like the tides
You are the night that calms my tired spirit
And the day that fills my heart with joy
You are my Muse, My Goddess, My Friend
And I would wait many lifetimes
To have that one perfect moment
When we can be together
Always remember that I love you
With no conditions or demands
I will still be here weeks, months, years
With love in my heart and arms open wide
With a patience born from my knowing
That one day we will have our perfect moment

Terry Dobson

What do you see?

What do you see when you look at me
The smile, the laughter, the eyes
Do you see the tears that I hide
Do you see the darkness inside
Do you see the dragon I have battled all my life
Do you see me happy
Or do you see beyond the laughter to the pain

Did you know there are times I cry
Times I feel so alone
Times I wish that death would claim me for his own
To end this life once and for all
To ease the pain and loneliness
To cast a final curtain
And wrap me in my shroud

But I don't give in to the darkness
I fight it every day
In every way

But do you see it in me
Lurking in the shadows
Gnawing on the bones
Sucking the marrow
Stealing my strength
Seducing me with its whispers of peace

But each time I stand up and face it down
Naked and cold, weak as I am
Wrapped in chains
I take those chains in my hands
And strike the dragon down each time
Forcing it to retreat for a while

Still I know it's there
I can feel its stare
Feel its hunger
The heat of its rage
But for now I'm free
Released from my cage
I turn my back, stand tall
And walk into my future

Terry Dobson

Haunted

She is on my mind again
The play of sunlight on her hair
Her smile, gentle and sweet
Strikes like lightning out of a clear sky
Piercing me through to my soul
Leaving my heart naked and scared
Shivering in the palm of her hand
Hers to hold forever
Or to crush with a word
Each random thought
Spirals back to her
To the spark in her eyes
That sets my soul aflame
To the sound of her voice
As it caresses my ear
To the touch of her hand
That makes me tremble
From love and from fear
Can she sense the turmoil
That rages hot inside me?
And even though I'm here alone
Her presence lingers
In my heart and mind
I can still sense her
Still feel her touch
Her scent forever with me
Unforgettable
Haunting me
Taunting me
To gaze into her eyes
To tell her what I want to say
"I love you"
And risk her walking away

First Published in *Footprints at the Water's Edge: More Tales from Easington Writers*, edited by Terry Dobson, 2011

Silent screams

I scream, but all is silent
No breath in my lungs
No heartbeat to pump the blood
That drains into Mother Earth
To feed the soil, the plants, the worms

Huge and grim, the crow sits upon my chest
Razor beak tears at my flesh
Plucks out my eye
And I scream but there is no sound

I die, yet I lie here
Trapped in this fleshy prison
Conscious and aware

Blue lights chase the crow
Tramp of feet
Flashes of light
Of photos being taken
The scene of the crime
At last I move
But not under my control
Lifted into a rubber bag
Zipped up
Alone in darkness
Blacker than night

So is this death?
An eternity of silent screaming

Terry Dobson

Light returns
The silver of the scalpel
As it slices the flesh from my bones
Snap, snap, snap
As my ribs are cut
And all the while
My silent cries
No please, I'm here, can't you see
It's me, I'm still in here!

But they cannot hear
My voice has gone
And I can do nothing
But watch as they strip my organs
Like pieces of meat
Heart, lungs, liver
Weighted and measured
A commentary on how I had lived
And theories on my death
Then stitch up my carcass
And slide me in the fridge
Until they come for me

They dress what is left
And seal me inside the casket
Seal me for eternity in darkness
But I don't feel dead
I am still aware
Still screaming
Wanting to bang upon the lid
Wanting release
Not to be here

I hear the soil upon the lid
As they bury my remains
Until there is nothing but silence

If this is a dream
Why can't I wake?
Is this what death is?
To lie here as the flesh rots
Forever alone in the grave
The only sound the worms that feast
And my silent screams
An eternal nightmare
Buried and dead, yet somehow alive

Terry Dobson

Our love

The sun shone down
Like a gilded idol
Showering us, cleansing us

Our souls fly high
Like great eagles searching for prey
But the prey of our souls
Was to pray for our souls
To be united in eternal love

One kiss and we are lost
Lost in a paradise never before discovered
A paradise created in the light of love
A love so pure and simple
So beautiful and true
Eternal and undying
Natural like you

The hunt

Naked trees, frozen forest
Leached of colour,
Grey and white
Ice pops, crackles
Branch explodes
As fear-driven feet
Push through snow
Heart thumps
Panic-stricken
As death stalks,
Hunger-fuelled desperation
Behind, a shadow
Swift strong jaws
Teeth like swords
Pierce hamstring
Slash throat
Torn flesh
Bright red bursts
On frozen white
Grisly winter blossom
Bloody muzzle raised
Calls the pack
To feed, to live
A while longer

Terry Dobson

There were always times

There were always times
When the darkness consumed me
Rising from the depths of my mind
Like some predator it strikes
To lay bare my flesh
And tear at my life

There were always times
When sunshine faded
Turning my world into black and grey
When the words I write
Are born from pain
As the colour bleeds away

There were always times
When my pillow was wet
As it soaked up the salt of my tears
When the world turned against me
In my own paranoia
And left me alone with my fears

There were always times
When my heart filled with sorrow
And I felt unloved and unclaimed
Like an orphan discarded
With no wolves to raise me
Lost in the woods I remained

There were always times
When I was blinded
Couldn't see the good for the bad
Alone with my nightmares
Scream at the darkness
And no relief to be had

I was forged in the darkness
In the blackest of storms
My spirit was the heat in the night
Like a sword I was tempered
To be stronger than steel
I emerged as a weapon for light

There were always times
When I rose from the darkness
With love in my soul and my heart
No evil can diminish
The light that I bear
Even when my life falls apart

Terry Dobson

With open hearts

With open hearts and open minds
We open ourselves to something new
With open hearts and open minds
We open our eyes and see things anew

With open hearts and open minds
With a ready smile and a healing laugh
With open hearts and open minds
We set our feet on the healing path

With open hearts and open minds
We hear the beat of the healing song
With open hearts and open minds
Though we are many we are also One

Sacrifice

Impaled upon the tree of life
Blood slowly stains the bark
Pain throws off illusion
And I see the truth so stark

For nine days and nine nights
I hang upon that windswept tree
A sacrifice unto myself
Explore my own reality

Thought and Memory sustain me
Feed my ever craving mind
Cast their light upon my life
To show me where I had been blind

With new eyes I see myself
Through blood and pain reborn
I clutch the wisdom I have found
And from the tree I'm torn

I touch the earth and send down roots
I stand and reach up to the sky
In my heart I hold my truth
With my hands I cast away the lie

Before I leave this wilderness
I bow down unto the tree
With thanks I say one last goodbye
Before I march into eternity

Terry Dobson

Look at him now

Look at him now, see how he smiles
You'd never know that inside he's crying
Look at him now, see how he laughs
You'd never know that inside he's dying
Look at him now, see how he talks
You'd never know that inside he feels all alone
Look at him now, see how he dances
You'd never know that inside he's running scared

He won't let you close enough to see into his eyes
His heart is shattered, locked away in solid ice
He won't let you see his darkness and his pain
Too afraid some woman will break him once again
If you reach out a hand and offer him a smile
He'd jump and he'd run a hundred miles
Too scared to let you in, to let you mend his heart
Afraid that if he loves you he'll be torn apart

So he lives his life with his soul drowning
As it sinks in the depths of an oceanic loneliness

Look at them now, see through their eyes
For they'll never tell you what suffering they hide
Look at them now, see beyond the masks
They're lonely, forgotten, and broken inside
Put two of them together and they could make a whole
But they'll never know

Waking thoughts

When I wake my first thought is of you
I smile as I think of your smile
And the magic in your eyes
I sigh as I think of your touch
And your hand in mine
I hear spring in your voice
Bringing light into my life
Feeling my heart open
When I close my eyes
I hear the sea, and feel the sand
And I know that the beach
Will always remind me of you

Terry Dobson

Thoughts of the sea

Sadness blue as summer sky
Gentle sigh of the sea
Soothes the grieving mind
And lets the thoughts flow free

Mood black as night-time shadow
Whispering of the sea
Exorcises the haunted mind
And lets the thoughts flow free

Anger red as fresh spilled blood
Cleansing waves of the sea
Calms the raging mind
And lets the thoughts flow free

First Published in *Shrugging Off the Wind: Tall Tales from Easington Writers*, edited by Wendy Robertson and Avril Joy, 2010

Full moon rising

Tonight
As the full moon rises over the sea
I shall be there with you by my side
Arm in arm, or hand in hand
Wrapped in warmth upon the sand
Basking in the glow
Of the Moon in all its glory
Our ruler shining bright
Blessing us with her light
There is nowhere else I would rather be
Than there with you beside the sea

Terry Dobson

To love and light

The crow
Black and mournful
Cries out its lonely call
My heart
Alone and breaking
Beats out a funeral march
My body
Cold and naked
Shivers in the cold still air
My soul
Lost and yearning
Seeks shelter from the darkness
You smile
Loving and warm
A beacon to outshine the sun
The crow
On wings of night
Flies off with cries of joy
My heart
Alive and whole
Beats out a dance of love
My body
Warm once more
Would give up life for you
My soul
Search fulfilled
Gently floats in love and light
You are
My one true love
Who saved me from myself

Happy Valentine's Day

I was lying in the desert sands,
A seed lain dormant and forgotten
Then you came like a shower of rain
Woke me up and I began to bloom
Now I stretch up to the sky
My face filled with hope
My heart filled with warmth
My dreams filled with your smile
I know we've barely taken a step
On the road to the future
But I'm not afraid to reach out
To take your hand in mine
I look forward so much
To getting to know you
Welcome into my life
And Happy Valentine's Day

Terry Dobson

I offer myself

I let loose control of my emotions
Freed from the chains that protect me
They drift like clouds upon the winds
And I stand before you naked and vulnerable
A supplicant before your beauty and grace
As I gaze into your eyes, tears begin to fall
For the first time I see what I have longed for
Yet could never find while I hid behind walls
Shielded from harm, yet never truly living
Never taking the risk of allowing love through
In the false belief that my heart
Could not thus be broken
Yet my soul yearned for that love
That light that brings life
And then you came
And I knew it was time
To cast off those bindings
To take the risk
And allow myself to love
To offer myself
With an open heart
To you

Blessed day

I close my eyes and my senses come alive
Leaves murmur and tickle one another
And in their joy I hear your name
A gentle summer breeze passing through
Tousles my hair and tugs my shirt
And in its play I can feel your touch
A rippling stream creates a melody
Which it sings as it flows by
And in its song I hear your voice
On such a beautiful day
Surrounded by the delights nature can bestow
How could I not think of you?
You are with me always now
You live in my heart, part of my soul
And so I carry you with me
To share in my life, in the wonders I see
You are the flowers, the leaves, the trees
The rippling stream, the birds and the breeze
Your spirit surrounds me day and night
Filling my life with beauty and light
Thank you
I love you
My friend
My delight

First Published in *Footprints at the Water's Edge: More Tales from Easington Writers*, edited by Terry Dobson, 2011

Terry Dobson

Was your love ever real?

Love still flows within my blood
I feel it with every breath I take
But what once felt so sweet to me
Is causing my heart to break

There was a time we were so close
It felt like nothing could keep us apart
But was it all just a game to you
Were you merely playing a part?

Was your love ever real
Cos that's not how it feels
As I cry here alone in the night
I gave you my love
But it wasn't enough
Now you've stolen away with my life

You've taken my sunlight
You've shattered my dreams
No word of goodbye
Just vanished it seems

All I have left
Is the love in my heart
It tears me apart
What happened to us?
I just don't know
Where did you go?

Was your love ever real
Cos that's not how it feels
As I cry here alone in the night
I gave you my love
But it wasn't enough
Now you've stolen away with my life

I love you so
I love you still
I love you now
I always will

Was your love ever real
Cos that's not how it feels
As I cry here alone in the night
I gave you my love
But it wasn't enough
Now you've stolen away with my life

Terry Dobson

Love's light

Burn a candle and in the pale dancing light
Watch the flickering shadows of humanity
As they hover on the edge of darkness
But the light of love that is inside your heart
Can be brighter than the Sun
If you can only learn to use it right
The flame of love will burn on and on
Casting out the shadows
Driving back the dark
Sending out a beacon to the lost and lonely
Love can light up the Earth and bring warmth in Winter
Open your heart and let it through
Rejoice in the natural wonder and truth
And the selfless emotion of love

The circle

The circle
It has no beginning and no end
It is equal, symmetrical and uncorrupted
It is the Whole for which we all must strive
In all ways

The circle
Its strength is its power
It has no weak points
It gave birth to the wheel of life
That never stops turning
The symbol of Eternity.

Terry Dobson

Something beautiful

Something beautiful was born that night
As we lay together beneath the stars
And I feel it growing stronger day by day

It came suddenly and burst into life
And feels so pure like a divine flame
So perfect and true within my heart and soul

So amazing and new that I found my tears
So powerful it took my breath away
And without it I will never be whole again

And though tonight I lie here alone
I can feel you always here with me
My lover, my teacher, my student, my best friend

Didgeridoo

Moan and drone
Continuous breath
Providing momentum
To hum on the lips
Transform to sound
Breath must be round
To keep on playing
The didgeridoo
In through the nose
Out through the mouth
A steady stream of air
Always exhaled
Held in cheeks
While breathing in
Over and over
The circle begins
But never ends
Until the mind
Says quit

Terry Dobson

Rainbow of my heart

Rainbow of my heart
You always shine so bright
A smile to wipe away my tears
In the darkest hours of the night

Rainbow of my heart
You glow with love and light
A flame to warm and guide me
In the coldest hours of the night

Rainbow of my heart
You put my fears to flight
My love for you sustains me
In the lonely hours of the night

Heart laid bare

Sunlight, golden and bright
Reveals my soul, my fragile heart
A great capacity to love
But the fear remains of great pain
Yet from pain comes growth
As birthing pains bring joy and life
And if she should be my true soulmate
Do I have the strength of will to break through
The walls I've taken years to build around me?
To stand naked and open to truth and love
With light shining on me and through me
To offer myself up to the one with whom
I could walk hand in hand through eternity

Terry Dobson

The way I feel

I didn't realise how lost I was
As I wandered the landscape of my life
Until you danced into view
A glowing vision of beauty
That guided my steps
From that moment to this
I have begun to realise
Just how much I have missed
While I stumbled blindly onward
Without love by my side
But now I see more clearly
With colours so vivid and true
The air I breathe seems more pure
The sunshine gentle and golden
I cannot help but smile
At the newfound emotions
That play with my senses
And lighten my soul
Each day I feel more deeply
The bond that grows between us
I feel your presence always
As you inhabit my thoughts
And I allow myself to feel
The way I do about you

Footprints

Footprints at the water's edge
The waves sweep in and steal them
Erasing all trace they were ever there
But I know, I saw them
You, too, have left prints
Indelible on my heart
And neither time nor tide
Will ever take them
Whatever the future may bring
You will always have a place
Within my soul and my dreams
You are part of me now

First Published in *Footprints at the Water's Edge: More Tales from Easington Writers,* edited by Terry Dobson, 2011

Terry Dobson

Beach banks

Early morning, peaceful
Rabbits graze, wary, watchful
A blur of stoat or weasel
Too quick to tell
Sun shines, larks sing
Nests in wild grasses and flowers
Where once stood spoil heaps
Tall, dark, barren
Now green for miles
The land dips and rises
Nature in control once more
Building a beautiful landscape
North over the fields and shrubs
Lies Easington, look there's Beacon Hill
South I see Blackhall, Crimdon,
Hartlepool and more
On the edge, looking down
The sea, calm today, is gentle
As it tastes the pebbles
On the beach
The waves kissing the land
As they have for time immemorial
In and out, powerful, eternal
The breathing of the Earth itself

Something happened to me

I used to be lost, I used to be alone
But I was so blind in the dark I didn't realise
But then I felt your hand take mine
And then I was lost in your eyes
When I caught a glimpse of paradise

Now I feel I can fly, reach out so high
I feel I can soar, and dance among the stars
I hear music in your voice as it whispers out my name
I feel you always even when we're apart
I feel you always in my heart

Something happened to me
Something happened to me
Something happened to me when I met you

I see rainbows dancing in your smile
I see the colours so bright and true
I see the beauty you've brought into my life
Everything feels so shining and new
I love you

The feel of your skin against mine
Gets me higher than the finest wine
When I hold you close to me
I feel more alive than I've ever been
I ache so much
When I feel your touch
Passion sets me on fire
Filling me with desire
I would fall on my knees
To give you what you need

Something happened to me
Something happened to me
Something happened to me when I met you
I fell in love with you

Terry Dobson

More than love

In the past I've loved a girl or two,
But I've never met a girl like you,
You make me feel so good.
And when we hold each other oh so tight,
Bodies touching and it feels oh so right,
Passion burning through my blood.

I thought I'd been in love before,
But girl this is so much more
Than I have ever had
And it makes me glad.
And when I tasted our first kiss
I knew I'd never felt like this.
I need you so bad.

It's more than love
I more than love you
I more than need you
More than words can say

It's more than love
I more than love you
I more than need you
Much more every day

I thought that I'd seen everything
Until you taught my heart to sing
And so much more
Than I knew before.
I thought I knew what loving meant
Then you came and you were heaven sent
You shook me to my core,
Knocked me to the floor.

I feel that I'd fight dragons for you
I'd even brave the fires of hell
To look into your eyes
Or just for one more smile.
Something's burning up my soul
Something I just can't control
Can't fight the fire
Of my desire

It's more than love
I more than love you
I more than need you
More than words can say

It's more than love
I more than love you
I more than need you
Much more every day

It's more than love
I more than love you
I more than need you
More than words can say
Much more every day

Terry Dobson

Rhythm of love

I hear the drum in my heart
I feel the love in my soul
I hear the flute in your voice
I feel the silk of your skin
I hear you sigh in the night
I feel the rhythm get faster
I hear my voice call your name
I feel my spirit fly free
I hear your body call me
I feel our souls become one
I hear my heart like a drum
I feel that heart filled with love
I hear my destiny call
I feel you right there beside me
I hear the drum in my heart
I feel the love in my soul

The face

In the crowd I saw today
The face that has haunted me all of my life
The face I first saw as a child
In those black and white photos I found in the attic
I remember that face
And those cold, staring eyes that made me scream
They still watch me now
Leer from the darkness when I'm lost in my dreams
But today was no dream
I was out on the street when I felt its stare
Cold but hypnotic
And I stopped still
Caught up in its snare
Then came the smile
The icy whisper as it drew the knife
No more nightmares
The face gone at last
Along with my life

Terry Dobson

The moon and you

The Moon, my ruler,
I feel its pull
I feel its power
Energising
And now there's you
I feel your pull
I feel my attraction
Hypnotising

The crystal

Hard and gleaming
Gaze, see the translucent colours
So many beautiful colours
That can never be copied
Only imagined

See the burning light of healing and love
An eternal flame
The spirit inside calls to you
Through the mist
The singing spirit
The Faerie that dances around the flame
So happy
So lovely to behold
Feel the peace
And, though cold, the warmth
Of healing love

Terry Dobson

Prayer to you

One touch
I am shivering inside
One kiss
There's nowhere I can hide
The walls I spent years building
Could not stand against your hand
They fell apart at my desire
And crumbled into sand
As I looked deep into your eyes
I felt hope and glimpsed paradise
Now every time I see you
I want to fall to my knees
Call out your name
Offer myself as sacrifice
I hear the Goddess speak to me
She wears your face
She smiles your smile
She haunts my dreams
And answers all my prayers
I never want this feeling to end
Amen

First Published in *Footprints at the Water's Edge: More Tales from Easington Writers,* edited by Terry Dobson, 2011

A year of loving you

Almost a year now since our first date
The February chill forgotten as we held hands
You taught me how to trust again
As I opened my heart to let you in
You taught me how to breathe
How to live and how to love
How to talk and how to listen
And how to be silent in the moment
I allowed myself to be vulnerable
As I fell in love with you
I still love you, though we have drifted
But time has no meaning to the way I feel
And I will wait lifetimes for the chance
To spend one perfect moment with you
To hear your voice
To feel your touch
To tremble beneath your fingertips
To taste your kiss
To tell you that I love you
My soul mate, my love, my teacher, my friend

Terry Dobson

We and the moon

As the moon shone down upon the sea
She turned her gazed to you and me
We talked and laughed into the night
We smiled and kissed beneath her light
We felt her touch as we held hands
She gave us blessings upon those sands
A magical presence in the air
A special night that we both shared

Spring in your eyes

I think of you as I gaze out to sea
And in the sunlight shimmering
On the pale blue waters of reflected skies
I see the sparkle of your eyes
As I hear the birds all around me
Singing joyfully in their courtship
Tender notes that reach out to the skies
I see the beauty of your eyes
I think of you as I sit overlooking the sea
In the warmth of the golden springtime sun
That shines down from the clearest skies
I see the magic in your eyes
I feel the softest breeze on my cheek
And for a moment I imagine it is your breath
And as I turn my face towards the skies
I see the Goddess in your eyes

Terry Dobson

Shadow and light

I dwell in the shadows
Alone in the night
Darkness all around me
Grasps me tight
Feels like the hand of Death
With the chill of the grave
I shiver with icy tears
Shackled like a slave

Then a spark
Shines through the night
Growing stronger
Bursts with light
The shadows howl
And then they flee
Let loose the chains that bind
Suddenly I'm free

I feel a lover's warmth
Take the chill from my bones
I feel a lover's touch
As it gently leads me home
I feel a lover's lips
On the kiss that saves my life
I feel a lover shield me
And save me from the knife

Now I dwell in your light
As I worship at your feet
I feel your tender touch
You make my life complete
You have banished my shadows
Now I need no place to hide
I only need a smile
From my lover and my guide

First Published in *Footprints at the Water's Edge: More Tales from Easington Writers,* edited by Terry Dobson, 2011

You are my Goddess

You are my Goddess
Whose heart and hands
Have healed my body and soul
You have given me love
I had never dreamed could be
I feel my love for you
In every depth of my being
I give thanks each day
That you are not just part of my life
But so much more
I wish for you only good things
May this and every other day
From this moment on bring you joy

About the Author

Terry Dobson was born in 1965 and has lived all of his life around the coast of County Durham in north east England. He is a member of Easington Writers and of Blackhall Writers, and has had poems and short stories published in both of Easington Writers' anthologies. Terry has also had short stories published in *Scarlet Magazine*. In his mid-life crisis he is learning how to play didgeridoo and is training to be a counsellor.

Printed in Great Britain
by Amazon.co.uk, Ltd.,
Marston Gate.